Whodunits You Can See

Picture Puzzle Mysteries

Written and illustrated by
Rolf Heimann

Sterling Publishing Co., Inc.
New York

Library of Congress Cataloging-in-Publication Data

10 9 8 7 6 5 4 3 2 1

Published by Sterling Publishing Company, Inc.
387 Park Avenue South, New York, NY 10016
© 2003 by Rolf Heimann
The material in this book has been excerpted from: *For Eagle Eyes Only* ©
Rolf Heimann 1989; *More for Eagle Eyes* © Rolf Heimann 1990; and
For Eagle Eyes Again © Rolf Heimann 1998, all published by Roland Harvey Books
Distributed in Canada by Sterling Publishing
c/o Canadian Manda Group, One Atlantic Avenue, Suite 105
Toronto, Ontario, Canada M6K 3E7

Printed in Hong Kong

Sterling ISBN 1-4027-0262-0

CONTENTS

How to Use This Book

You don't need a magnifying glass to solve any of the puzzles
in this book. But you do need sharp eyes and some time
and patience.

Read the story, then try to solve the mystery. When you
read the answer, you'll find that it asks more questions than it
answers! So, close the bedroom door, sharpen up your eagle
eyes, and get ready to conquer the mysteries that lie ahead.
Good luck!

Find the Thief

The king was furious. He had ordered his cook to bake him four blackberry pies, but when he came to get them, there were only three.

"I'm so sorry," the cook said. "I went down to the cellar and when I came back, one pie was gone."

"Bring all the servants who have been in the kitchen today," roared the king. "I will question them!"

All the servants said they were innocent. The maid said she was on a diet. The scrubwoman said she hated blackberries. The coachman said he had just come in for a drink of water, and the kitchen boy said he wouldn't dare take anything after the beating he'd gotten last time.

"Silence!" screamed the king. "First you steal my pie, then you tell me a pack of lies! If none of you will tell me who the thief is, I'll have all your heads chopped off!"

Can you save the lives of the servants? Look carefully and you'll find the thief.

Answer on page 72.

Find the Sandals

"Hey, hurry up," Karl called to his sister. "I can hear the ice-cream truck!"

The ice-cream truck passed the campgrounds only once a day, and the children hated to miss it.

"Wait for me!' cried Sherry. "Mom—where are my sandals?"

The path was full of stones and thistles and Sherry did not want to go barefoot. Her mom had no idea where the sandals were. "It's about time you learned to take care of your things," she said. "And hurry up or you'll miss out on the ice cream...."

Sherry was in trouble. The camp was a jumble, but with sharp eyes, you can spot the two sandals.

Answer on page 72.

The Exploding Planet

Ben Gibson, chief engineer of the interstellar supply depot Trivia III, came racing up the hill on his jet crawler.

"This planet is about to explode," he said. "Luckily, Smithy is nearly finished with the repairs to our escape module."

"How nearly finished?" asked the workers who were very alarmed. "He was nearly finished days ago!"

"I see you understand how serious the situation is," answered the chief engineer. "I want you to find another one of these binary flow control ducts. Smithy threw one out the other day but now he needs it. The sooner you find it, the earlier we'll be able to get away."

Chief engineer Gibson is right. Trivia III is about to blow up. Only if the missing part is found in time can the crew get away, so don't stop until you find it! Every second counts!

Answer on page 72.

4

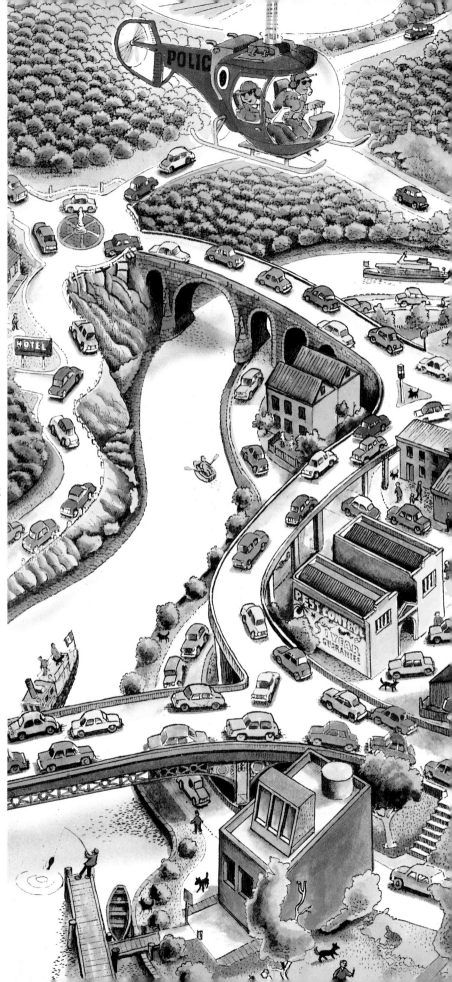

Spot the Getaway Car

Katie Mason, police pilot, directed the helicopter towards the city's biggest bank building. She had received a radio message saying that armed robbers had stolen half a million dollars and escaped in a green car.

"A green car!" called co-pilot Hannah Smith in despair. "There must be hundreds of green cars in the city. We're never going to find the right one!"

"We might be able to," said Mason. "The car in question has red wheels. There can't be many cars like that around! If we can spot it and radio its position to the ground, the police can put up road blocks and arrest these guys."

If the helicopter crew's eyes are as good as yours, they're bound to find the car pretty soon!

Answer on page 72.

Spot the Ring

It was the wedding of the year. Sylvia Weatherton-Smythe, daughter of the Earl of Worcestershire, was to marry Freddie Bloggs, heir to a billion-dollar tomato-sauce empire. All the newspapers and television stations were covering the event.

But when it was time to put the wedding band onto the bride's finger, the ring could not be found. Both groom and best man turned their pockets inside out. No ring.

The guests in the back craned their necks, and those in front began to giggle. Sylvia blushed deeply.

"I've never been so humiliated," she hissed. "If you don't find the ring in one minute, the wedding is off. I'd rather stay single forever than marry such a fool!"

You've spotted the ring already, haven't you?

Answer on page 72.

Help Ashley Survive

Ranger Ashley Stumbleberg
felt like crying. He had been
sent into the Grand Canyon to
do a wildlife survey, but just as
he'd started to count the little
gray squirrels, his burro had
gone off and left him without
any equipment. What would
he do without his binoculars
and his notebook? How could
he survive without water, his
flour, and his blanket? His
favorite frying pan, the one
with the brown handle, was
gone, too.

   If only he could find his
burro—or at least the six most
important pieces of his
equipment. . . .

**Can you help him find
them?**

Answer on page 72.

7

Fish or Chicken?

The Malone family was traveling by car through Germany.

"I'm hungry," said Willy as his father pulled the car over to the side of the road. "Look, there's a seafood restaurant. Let's go there."

"I hate fish," objected his sister Isabel. "Let's have chicken. There's a chicken place over there!"

"Why can't you two ever agree about anything?" asked their father. "But before we do anything else, I want to find a gas station. After I fill up the car, we'll go and eat at the first restaurant we come to. No arguments."

"Just watch out for these foreign roads," their mother pointed out. "Some of them are one-way streets."

Will they have seafood or chicken for dinner?

Answer on page 73.

Help Yill Help Yack

Deep in the foothills of the Himalayas, there lived two children, Yack and Yill. One day Yack became very ill and his sister went to the local healer.

"I'm afraid," said the wise old man, "that there is nothing I can do for your brother. To save him we need a certain herb that grows in a very special place up in the mountains. It's called *superfluensis floribundis*, or redwort for short. Alas, I'm too old and feeble to make the journey to get it."

"I'll get it!" cried Yill. "Just tell me where to find it and what it looks like!"

"I can do better than that," said the healer. "Here, take this picture."

When Yill arrived at the place in the mountains, she was amazed at the variety of plants.

Will she find the herb that can save her brother? It will be dark soon, and there is no time to lose. Help her—you'll have a friend for life!

Answer on page 73.

Find the Wolf!

"Grandmother," cried Little Red Riding Hood, "why do you have such small eyes? And such a small nose? And such tiny ears?"

"What do you expect?" asked her Grandmother, eyeing the basket the girl had brought with her. "And speak up, I can hardly hear you!"

"Why do you have such a small mouth—without any teeth in it?" shouted LRRH at the top of her voice.

"Good heavens, girl, not so loud! Do you want the wolf to hear you? By the way, have you seen him today?"

"No, I haven't," answered LRRH.

"Well, go find him. I left a dish of oatmeal in the garden for him. We don't want him walking around being hungry—no telling what he might do...."

Help LRRH find the wolf. He's somewhere in the woods.

Answer on page 73.

Where's the Camera?

Lizzie and Timmy were having a picnic at their favorite watering hole when they heard a big splash in the water. They looked up and couldn't believe their eyes.

"What is it?" cried Timmy in amazement. "Is it a dragon? Or the Loch Ness monster?"

"It—it looks like a dinosaur or something," said Lizzie. "And look what it's done to our boat! We'll get blamed for that for sure. What are we going to do?"

"Nobody will believe us," agreed Timmy, "unless we can get this on film. Where is our camera?"

They had brought a camera along, but in the excitement, they couldn't remember where they had put it.

In a few minutes the monster will slip back into the water, never to be seen again. Is that enough time to find the camera?

Answer on page 73.

11

Find Ginger!

"Did you see Ginger?" asked Laura. "I can't find him anywhere!"

Laura's father, who was about to shovel away the freshly fallen snow, paused in his work. "He can't be far," he said. "Have you looked in the kitchen?"

"I looked everywhere!" Laura cried. "The poor thing will freeze to death if he's outside. It's so cold today!"

Ginger was Laura's kitten, and she loved him more than anything else in the world.

"Why don't you go and check the upstairs window in your room?" suggested Laura's father. "You know how Ginger loves jumping out onto the roof of the woodshed."

If Ginger had jumped out of the upstairs window, his tracks should be visible in the fresh snow.

Follow those paw prints now, before the snow is cleared away!

Answer on page 73.

Can You Save Your Life?

The pirate captain was grinning. He had not only captured rich treasure, but also a little kid named Tom— the son of his worst enemy.

"You, boy," growled the pirate, "will be shark bait before the sun goes down!"

"Captain, sir," said Tom, trying to conquer his fear, "you ought to ask me a riddle, as a chance to save my life. That would be the sporting thing to do, sir."

"Sporting?" roared the pirate. "I know no riddles, but I like some sport. Tell you what—guess the name of my parrot, and you'll go free. What's more, if you guess right, you can have all the pieces of eight in my treasure chest."

"You've got to give me a hint," begged Tom.

"Very well, here's your hint. My parrot's name is like my dog's name, only backwards."

Tom thanked his lucky stars that his glasses were not broken during the fighting. His sharp vision saved his life. Would you be able to save yours?

Answer on page 73-74.

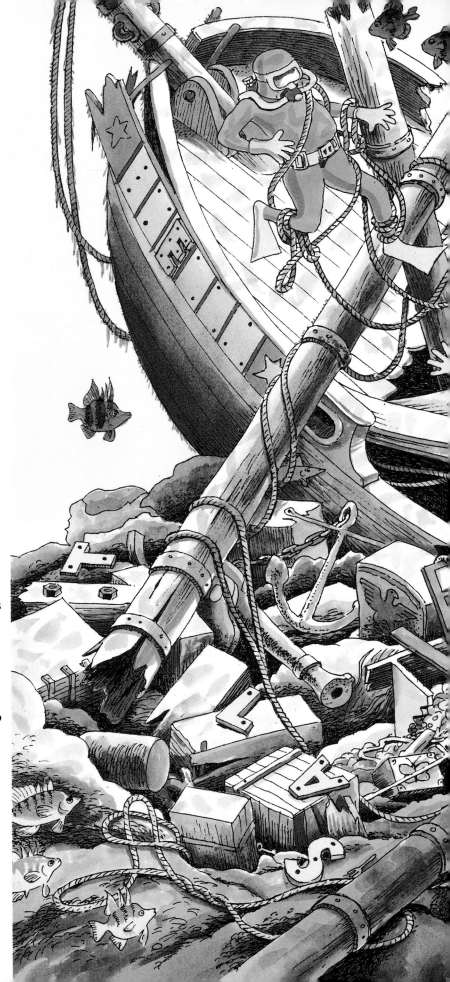

13

Where's the Knife?

Andy and Willy were expert divers, but even expert divers can get careless when they get excited. And the most exciting thing to a diver is the wreck of an old sailing ship like this one!

Andy was about to explore the darkness inside the wreck when he felt something pulling on his leg. At first, he thought it was a shark; he was relieved to see it was only a rope.

But the more he struggled, the more the rope tightened around his legs. This was serious! Luckily, Andy and Willy always dived together so they could help each other when one of them got into trouble. Andy gestured to his friend to cut the rope.

But where was Willy's knife? He had panicked and dropped it!

Help Willy to find his knife. It can't be far.

Answer on page 74.

Naming the Creature

Jessie and Hannah were pleased that Sir Pfifferstone had invited them along on a little expedition. They had never seen a forest like this!

"Yes, it's a totally unexplored country," explained Sir Pfifferstone proudly. "I've heard reports of a large beetle that looks like a leaf and of a butterfly that resembles pink snakeweed. If you are the first to discover them, I'll name them after you."

"Why do they call it pink snakeweed?" Hannah asked, glancing around nervously.

"Oh, that's because there are so many snakes around here. Watch out for them. Some of them are quite deadly...."

It took the girls only two minutes to discover the beetle and the butterfly. If you are quicker than they were, you can name them after yourself!

Answer on page 74.

15

Test the Fiendish Invention

"Stop where you are!" called McRob, the notorious thief. "I warn you, sir, that you cannot get inside my latest fiendish invention—the House of Security. If you dare to cut the strings, the balloons will rise and burst on the sharp nails above. This will wake my cat, Tiger, who will jump off the balance. The weight will then drop into the tank, which will make the water overflow and set in motion the deadly mechanism that will plunge you into my patented mixture of crocodiles, snakes, and scorpions. Beware!"

The king's musketeer hesitated for a moment and then said, "I do not fear your silly machine. It will not work as you say. To prove it, I will cut the strings and stay right here on the trap door!"

Would you be just as confident as the musketeer?

Answer on page 74.

Win Princess Rebecca

"I don't know much about art," said the king, "but I know what I like. I like my pictures to be lifelike. I just spent a lot of money on my new castle, and the least I expect from you fellows is that you get the number of windows and towers right. Whoever does the best job of that will marry my daughter, the lovely Princess Rebecca."

The painters took one good look at Princess Rebecca and decided to make a deliberate mistake so that they wouldn't have to marry her. Only one of the painters couldn't bring himself to make a mistake.

Which painter was it?

Answer on page 74.

37

17

Beat the Train

It had been fun riding the old steam train to Eaglestone. But now Michael and Michele meant to catch the 2:30 P.M. train to Lakeside.

"The train to Lakeside," announced the conductor, "will be an hour late."

"Oh, no," said Michael. "Our friends will be waiting for us. We told them that we'd be there at 3 o'clock. Is there a way we can get to Lakeside earlier?"

"Well," mused the conductor, "the bus leaves in ten minutes, but it takes twice as long as the train. That's because it makes so many stops. There is also the paddle steamer that leaves at 2:15. The steamer takes three times longer than the train."

What's the quickest way to Lakeside?

Answer on page 74.

39

Solve the Space Snafus

"I like hexagons," Dr. Celia Baker explained to her two guests. "As you can see, I designed HEX 2 in the shape of a hexagon, which means it has six sides and six corners."

Wendy and Jack agreed that the hexagons looked good.

"I like the way hexagons fit together," said Baker. "Bees build their hives in hexagons, did you know that? And snowflakes always crystallize as hexagons. Never with five or seven sides, always with six. Isn't that interesting?"

Dr. Baker pointed to a blue space station nearby. "That one was designed by Professor Pentus. He prefers pentagons. Sometimes our spare parts get mixed up. Oh, no—they've done it again! They sent us five-sided frames. I'll have to send them back and order new ones."

"Wait," said Jack. "Not all the frames are wrong. I can see some hexagons among them."

Jack was correct. How many of the frames were right and how many were wrong?

Answer on page 74-75.

Fix the Dinosaur

Kirsten and Ken were helping Professor Gruber in the construction of the museum's new dinosaur models. It was interesting work, though a bit scary at times. The models looked so lifelike!

They were cleaning up when Ken called out, "Oh, no, here are three parts left over. Professor Gruber is going to inspect our work in a minute. We'd better find out where these parts belong!"

"Not to worry," said Kirsten. "That won't take us long."

Would you be able to find where the parts go just as easily?

Answer on page 75.

TRICERATOPS

S

43

Spot the Santa

Lolly and Robert were trying to deliver an important letter to Santa Claus. To their dismay, they suddenly saw themselves surrounded by lots of men in red.

"Only one of them can be the real Santa Claus," whispered Lolly." The others must be his helpers."

"Or fakes," added Robert. "Let's try and spot the fakes. The real Santa Claus would never smoke. And he wouldn't wear anything but black boots. He wouldn't wear sunglasses or earrings or belt buckles with skulls. And he wouldn't read financial papers. He can't be skinny, and his cap must be reasonably floppy."

"You're right," agreed Lolly. "That leaves only one who could be real...."

Can you spot him, too?

Answer on page 75.

45

Spot the Glasses

Building a tree house can be fun, but not when you're in a wheelchair. Danny did what he could to help from the ground, calling out warnings, like "The window's crooked," or "A flying saucer's coming."

Danny was right! Before his eyes a strange spacecraft slowly descended, a ladder dropped, and two purple aliens climbed out.

"Greetings, Your Majesty," one said.

"My name is Danny Meyers. How come you speak English? And do you really have eyes all around your head?"

"We study language tapes," said the alien. "And yes, we do have six eyes, so we don't need rearview mirrors. That's why we're here, actually. I dropped my glasses. Have you seen a pair of hexagonal glasses by any chance?"

Danny had been looking at them all morning and wondering what they were. Do you see them?

Answer on page 75.

Why the Majeo?

"What are those kids doing here?" bellowed Matt, chief engineer of the Majeo team. "Is this a secret project or not? Get them out of here!"

"Oh, please, sir," said Patrick. "We only want to make a quick sketch of your plane for our school magazine and get some specs. We're not spies or anything."

"Well," said Matt, "in that case, go ahead. But don't put in anything about our propulsion system."

"Okay," Peggy said. "But why do you call the plane Majeo?

"Sorry," said Matt, "I can't tell you that. It is a secret project, after all."

After Patrick and Peggy watched for a while, they figured out how the plane got its name. Can you?

Answer on page 75.

49

Find the Tablet

What an incredibly interesting tomb they had found! Grave robbers had been there before, of course, and left it in a mess. But the tomb was still full of mysterious things.

Expedition leader Priscilla Stonnell was especially excited. "Look at this!" she called from the stairs. "If only this tablet were complete. I believe that the symbol on it is of special significance. Before you do anything else, please help me find the rest of the tablet."

The other parts are still somewhere in the tomb.

Can you find them?

Answer on page 75.

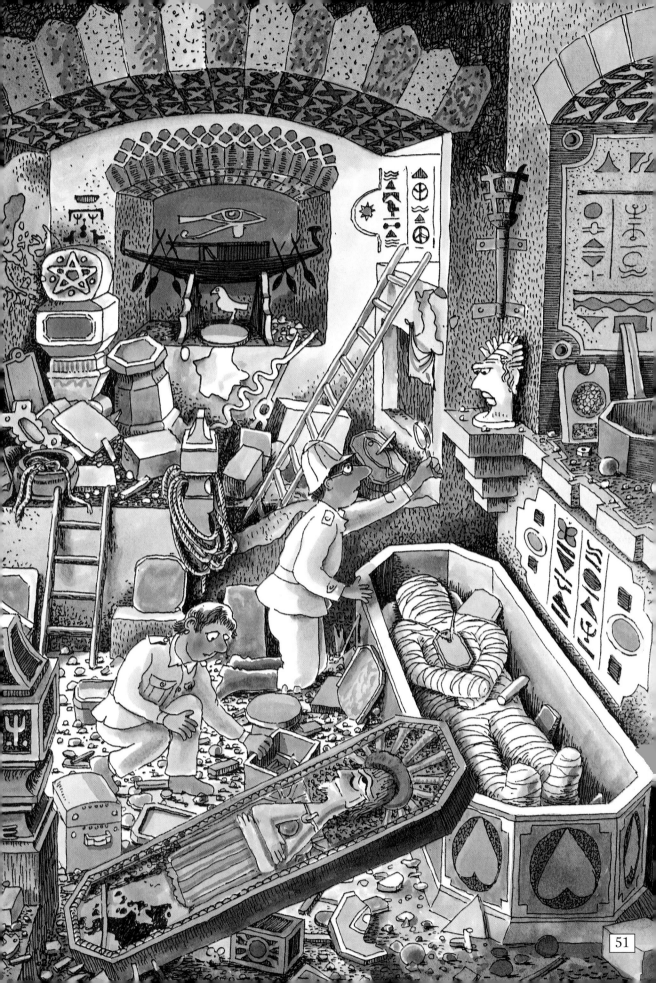

Find the Toothbrush

Ned and Ted had lost their way in the forest. Suddenly, they came upon a house—an unusual one made of gingerbread and sugar icing.

There was a witch standing in the doorway, rubbing her hands together. "Come on in, dear boys," she said, "Don't be shy. Help yourselves to some lovely sweets."

"No, thanks," said Ned. "We—er—didn't bring our toothbrushes, so we shouldn't have any. But we'd be grateful if you'd show us the way back to town."

"Never mind that," said the witch. "Have some sweets."

"Well, you obviously never use a toothbrush," said Ted, "and look at your teeth now!"

The witch quickly closed her mouth. She knew her teeth were not the best. "Oh, I do have a toothbrush," she said. "What's more, I'll lend it to you. Now, where did I put it?"

Ned and Ted could see the toothbrush, but they weren't going to help the witch find it. Do you see it?

Answer on page 75-76.

KUNST HONIG

53

25

Find the Tragic Mushroom

Once upon a time there were six little dwarves—Sloppy, Creepy, Nutty, Leaky, Bloopy, and Vladimir. Apart from their names, they had another problem. Every time they returned from a trip to the Tragic Mushroom Forest, they found that one of them had been bitten by a deadly Blue Adder.

Luckily, there was an effective treatment for the bite of the deadly snake. The antidote was made from a type of mushroom that could be recognized by the special arrangement of rings on its stem. The problem was that each time the dwarves went into the forest to get one of these special mushrooms, one of them got bitten, and they had to go back to the forest again...and again.

To end this vicious cycle, they decided to take home a second mushroom. The challenge was that it had to have the exact same pattern of rings as the one they had already chosen.

Can you help them find the right mushroom?

Answer on page 76.

Help the Genie

As Rich and Ruthie rubbed the dirt from an old bottle, the lid popped out and purple smoke began to pour out.

"You owe me three wishes," growled the giant genie. "If you don't fulfill them, I shall cut you into little pieces!"

"I think you've got it wrong," laughed Rich. "You owe us three wishes."

"No!" thundered the genie. "You rubbed me the wrong way! Listen carefully now."

"Your first wish is granted, master," Rich said, mocking the genie. "I'm listening."

"What? Oh, that didn't count," mumbled the genie.

"It counts when it's the other way around," said Rich.

"I wish you would stop interrupting me!" roared the genie. He immediately realized he had expressed another wish. Knowing that he had only one wish left, the genie said, "Listen. I've been in that tiny bottle for 1000 years! Find me another container! I don't care what it is as long as it has the colors of my turban—red, green, blue, and orange."

Rich and Ruthie could not find such a container, but they came up with another solution. Can you?

Answer on page 76.

27

Lowering the Noonball

Every day at noon, an iron ball was lowered from the Pink Tower so that the captains of all the ships in the harbor could set their clocks by it.

Lowering the noonball was a boring job, so Alexander Graham Hooper, Noonball Controller, made it more interesting by inventing a machine to do it for him. When he interviewed five applicants for the position of Assistant Noonball Controller, he gave them each a test.

"Watch closely," he said. "If I pop the balloon, the noise will scare Purple Nessie here so that she will pull the rope away. But if I lure her with this fish, she will come closer, making the rope go slack. Which should I do to make the noonball drop? The position of Assistant Noonball Controller will go to the first person who gives me the correct answer."

Which action will lower the noonball?

Answer on page 76.

The Disappearing Wallet

"Impossible!" cried Rita. You can't remove tattoos by hypnosis!"

"Go away, kid," said the owner of the shop, who did not want to lose a customer.

Roger, the biker, wanted to have the name "Lil" removed from his tattoo. "My new girlfriend's name is Nelly," he explained.

"We can do it while you wait," the owner said to Roger. "And it is almost painless. You'll merely feel a slight discomfort as my assistant applies the 'concussionette' to your cranial area."

Roger agreed and the assistant applied the concussionette to Roger's head.

"Ow!" cried Roger and passed out. When he came to, he looked down and said, "Hey, the name is still there!"

"Well, of course," said the assistant. "It takes two or three days for the letters to disappear. Image resistance, you know."

"Of course," said Roger, picking up his leather jacket. "How much do I owe you? Oh, I seem to have forgotten my wallet."

Rita could no longer contain herself. "Call the police," she said. "I'll tell them how your wallet disappeared!"

Do you know how the wallet vanished?

Answer on page 76.

Find the Leaf

The jungle of South Transmonia was a strange place. Take the Swallowtail glow worm, for instance. The red female could move only along the red branches of the Transmonian thorn-vine, while the green male could move only along green vines. If they made one step on a vine of the wrong color, they would suffer severe foot itch.

It was the glow worms' custom to meet at the full moon for a sing-along. The problem was that they had to meet each other on neutral ground—on a yellow leaf. Of course, this yellow leaf had to be reachable by both a red vine and a green vine.

Does such a leaf exist?

Answer on page 76.

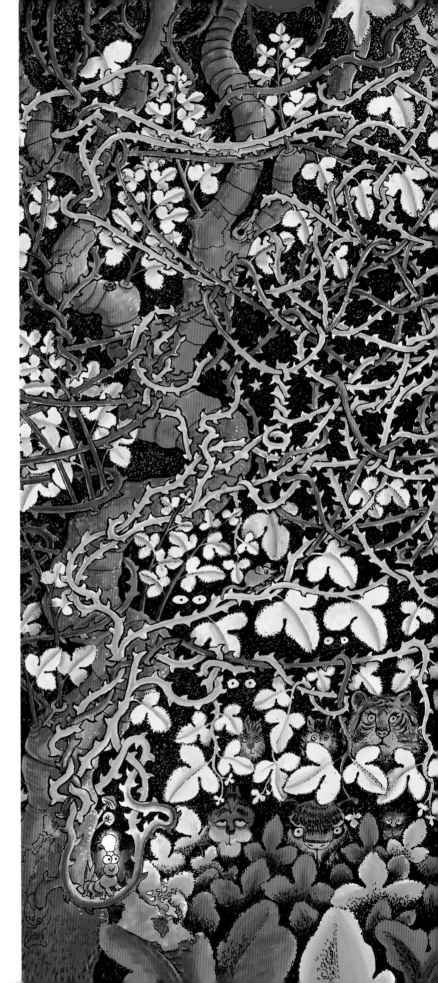

The Magic Carpet

Maia was the first to see the two aliens in their bright green flying saucer. "Hey, there!" she called. "I suppose you want us to take you to our leader?"

"Not at all," said the alien. "We've had bad experiences with leaders. We prefer the common people."

Maia's brother Mark spoke up. "I don't think you can call us common, since we're flying on a magic carpet."

"That's what I want to ask you about," said the alien. "What sort of fuel do you use for this craft?"

"This type of vehicle runs on pure imagination," explained Maia. "If you don't have imagination, forget it and stick to your ordinary saucers."

"We have imagination," said the alien. "Where can we buy one of these things?"

"You're in luck," said Mark. "We're flying right above the best magic-carpet market in the world. But don't buy just any carpet. Get one that has the same design and colors as ours. I think there's one left!"

Can you see the carpet Mark is talking about?

Answer on page 76.

Find the Right Berries

Arriving on the planet Turox, the astronauts Pete and Paul found some strange life forms: a chickenoid, a humanoid, and a tapewormoid. They switched on their Translatomatic and said, "We come in peace. We've heard about the great purple twinberries that grow here. Our mission is to check them out and take some home."

"Ah, those twinberries," said the chickenoid. "Most of them give you hallucinations."

"How can we tell which berries are good?" asked Pete.

"Not those that grow between green sections of the plant," said the humanoid. "They make you break out!"

"Can you tell us which of the berries are edible?" asked Paul politely. "We can't go back empty-handed."

"Only those that grow between red sections," said the tapewormoid. "But you'll be lucky to find any, since these are the ones we usually eat."

Would you be able to find the right berries?

Answer on page 76.

Food Festival

Emperor Krraak from the planet of Kkrrook was organizing an intergalactic food festival. The only foods still missing were sour pickles from Earth.

"Go to Earth and find a place called Spreewald," Krraak told his Royal Food Collector. "But don't bring back just any old sour pickles. If I remember rightly, the best ones come from a little farm that has a yellow flowering bush nearby and a stork's nest on the roof. Oh, and there are also a doghouse and a couple of pine trees. That's all I remember. Don't bring back pickles from anywhere else."

Can you find the place?

Answer on page 76.

Mixed-Up Times

It was the first time Tina had tried out her new time machine, and what a surprise she got when she slowed down for a soft landing!

"I can't believe it!" she cried. "Is this caveman riding a dinosaur? Something's wrong. Dinosaurs were extinct when people appeared on the earth."

She called out to the caveman, "What's your name?"

"Gloork," he answered. "I'll say there's something wrong. Your time machine is a dud."

"I put it together myself from a kit," said Tina.

"You must have your wires crossed," said Gloork "and because of that your time zones got all jumbled up. For instance, what about the saddle I'm sitting on? Saddles weren't invented until much later. If you look around, you'll see at least a dozen things that prove your time zones have been scrambled."

Can you find twelve or more things that are mixed up?

Answer on page 77.

Answers and Some More Questions

1. Find the Thief

After the silence that followed the king's threat, they suddenly heard slurping and licking and the chewing and gnashing of teeth. The sounds came from behind the oven, where a dog was eating the missing pie. The dog was one of the king's favorites, though, and wasn't punished too harshly.

After the king ate the remaining three pies, he got indigestion and asked for his medicine. But the chef had forgotten where he had put it. It was in a brown bottle with a red and green label. Can you find it?

Answer on page 78.

2. Find the Sandals

It took Sherry a few minutes to find her sandals. One was in the back of the car, the other in the tent. During her search, she also found her little sister's missing hairbrush. Can you find it, too?

Sherry was just about to rush after her mom when Karl came back, calling breathlessly, "Mom forgot her money. It's in her brown bag with the green handle!"

Fortunately, Sherry remembered seeing it in her search. Do you see it?

Answer on page 78.

3. The Exploding Planet

Fortunately, they found the missing part. It was near cart #6. But the chief engineer discovered another problem. He noticed that in the excitement, the hoses to the fuel tank had become entangled. If Fuel A was put into Tank B, there could be a disaster. Better check the hoses right away, before it is too late!

Answer on page 78.

4. Spot the Getaway Car

"I see it!" Mason called excitedly into the microphone. "A vehicle answering the description is proceeding north along the river. It's just going under the bridge!"

Within minutes, the police on the ground had stopped the getaway car and arrested the thieves.

"Well done," came the voice through the radio. "Return to base."

"Hey, while we're up here," Smith said, "let's look for my neighbor's lost dog."

"No way," laughed Mason. "We can't waste our time looking for lost dogs! You know what it costs to keep this machine in the air? Besides, we'd never recognize it from up here."

"I think we could. It's a black dog with a brown tail—very unusual. Look—there it is! I've spotted it already!"

Answer on page 78.

5. Spot the Ring

"A notorious jewel thief is among the guests," whispered Detective Sergeant Mary Lyndon to her assistant Dennis Dumboss.

"Why would they invite a jewel thief?" wondered Dumboss.

"He came uninvited, of course," snapped Lyndon, "and he's fiendishly clever. He usually hides stolen rings in flowerpots so that when he's searched he's always clean."

"How do you know it's a *he*?" asked Dumboss, trying to be clever.

"He's said to be bald," answered the detective. "And he always wears a red tie and a white carnation. Go and arrest him, Dumboss."

Dumboss hesitated. "There are some important people here," he said. "I wouldn't want to arrest the wrong person. I notice a few bald heads and red ties."

"As far as I can see," said Lyndon, "there is only one person here who answers the description. Go and arrest him now!"

Answer on page 78.

6. Help Ashley Survive

Luckily, Ranger Ashley Stumbleberg's eyes were as sharp as yours. As he looked around, he discovered his burro near Hylton Point, where its rope had snagged on an old tree stump. With great relief, Ashley also spotted his equipment scattered along the trail. But when he recovered his notebook, he realized that he had forgotten the number of squirrels he had just counted. Then Ashley had an idea. The number of squirrels was the same as the number of buttons on his jacket; all he had to do later was to count his buttons.

Answer on page 78.

7. Fish or Chicken?

After the family finished their seafood dinner, Willy suggested they visit Steinburg Castle. "It's a real German castle. Let's go there."

"That depends on how much it costs," said Willy's father thoughtfully. "I only have ten German marks left." (This all took place before the Euro took the place of the mark.) "We won't be able to get to a bank and exchange more money until later today. That may not be enough for the tickets."

"I remember seeing a sign where we stopped earlier today," said Isabel. 'DM' stands for German marks, doesn't it? And *erwachsene* means 'adults,' and *kinder* means 'children,' isn't that right?"

"That's right," agreed her mother.

"Well, I remember what it said on the sign. I think I can figure out whether we'll have enough money."

Answer on page 78.

8. Help Yill Help Yack

Curly the snail may have been as slow as other snails, but he certainly had sharper eyes. He could see up and ahead of him, half-hidden under some large leaves, a juicy specimen of his favorite food, which happened to be *superfluensis floribundis,* or redwort for short. He had already started his journey towards the plant when he realized that he was surrounded by the poisonous fungus yellowblight. If he so much as touched this fungus, he'd break out in a bad rash. It had happened before. Will Curly be able to reach the redwort without having to crawl over the yellowblight?

Answer on page 78.

9. Find the Wolf!

"You must be mistaken," said Professor Smark to his friend and colleague Dr. Hudson. "There are no wolves in this part of the world anymore."

"But there are, there are," cried Dr. Hudson excitedly. "I set a trap near the big oak tree by the brook and I caught one. It's there now—in my patented elevating wolf trap, up in the trees."

Professor Smark had his doubts. Stroking his beard, he said, "What you have caught is most likely a large domestic dog, my friend. Let me get my coat and my glasses and we'll investigate. Now, where are my glasses?"

"Well, you look for them, and then come on down to the big oak," called Dr. Hudson, as he ran down the hill.

"Easy for you to say," mumbled Professor Smark. "How can I look for my glasses when I can't see without them? I must have dropped them on my walk this morning."

He had indeed. He needs somebody with sharp eyes to find the glasses for him—you?

Answer on page 78.

10. Where's the Camera?

Lizzie remembered just in time that they had left the camera hanging on the handlebar of the bicycle near the pier. She was able to snap a photo just as the monster's tail disappeared into the water. The picture would probably show no more than a big splash and the outline of a dark object. Even so, they were anxious to get the film developed as quickly as possible. Then they discovered that the bicycle had a flat tire.

"Timmy, where's the bicycle pump?" she asked.

"How would I know?"

"You used it to pump up the ball, didn't you?"

The two began to argue. They would have been better off looking for the pump—it was right before their eyes!

Answer on page 78.

11. Find Ginger!

Laura discovered that she had left the window open in her room and tiny footprints showed that Ginger had escaped down the roof. Following Ginger's tracks, she saw that they led under the red door into the woodshed, where the kitten was curled up, warm and snug, on a nest of old rags. Ginger seemed to be warmer than Laura was!

Laura needed a good warm pair of mittens. Her grandmother had knitted her a pair for Christmas, but she had already lost them and was afraid to tell her parents she had. She still hoped the mittens would turn up.

Now, as she picked up Ginger, she noticed one of the mittens on a shelf in the woodshed. Where was the other one?

Answer on page 78.

12. Can You Save Your Life?

"Your parrot's name is Polly," said Tom confidently. He hoped he was right.

"Curses!" roared the pirate, gnashing his teeth. "The devil must have told you!"

Tom did not explain that he had spotted the dog's dish with its name on it near the main mast. Boldly, he asked that the pirate keep his promise and give him all the pieces of eight in his treasure chest. He knew they were valuable old Spanish coins.

The mean old captain now regretted his rash promise. "You misunderstood me, sonny," he said. "What I said was that you can have all the pieces with an eight on it. The joke's on you, boy!"

"Not so fast, captain," said Ernest. "First of all, give me your pants, since they've got the number eight on them." As he looked around, his keen eyes saw the number eight everywhere. He would be rich after all, provided the old pirate did not go back on his word again. (You never know, with pirates.)

Answer on page 78.

13. Where's the Knife?
Willy found the knife right behind the steering wheel. Quickly, he cut the rope and freed Andy. Together they continued exploring the wreck. They were interested in the name of the ship, but most of the letters had all fallen off. They could collect the letters, but how would they know the right order to put them in? Andy pointed to the screw holes in the hull. By comparing them with the holes in the letters, they worked out the name of the ship. Can you?

Answer on page 78.

14. Naming the Creature
The girls discovered the beetle and the butterfly on a tree trunk only a few paces to their right. Sir Pfifferstone took a step towards the tree, then gave a blood-curdling shriek. He had stepped on a snake, and the snake had bitten him.

"Oh, no," he groaned. "It's a deadly jumbo mamba! If we don't immediately rub pink snakeweed into the bite, I'll be dead in an hour!"

"Luckily, there's plenty of that around," said Jessie. "How many plants do you need?"

"Three will do," whispered Sir Pfifferstone, growing weaker by the minute. "But wait . . . don't take just any flower. Use only those with a black cross in the middle."

Answer on page 78.

15. Test the Fiendish Invention
With one stroke of his sword, the king's musketeer cut the strings. The balloons did rise and did wake up Tiger, who did jump off and did drop the weight, which did make the water overflow, and did make the wheel turn. But instead of pulling the support from the trap door, the string merely slackened. McRob had miscalculated the directions in which the wheels would turn.

"I arrest you in the name of the King!" said the musketeer. "And while I'm here, I'd better check out this place. The queen's crown is missing, too, and I wouldn't be at all surprised if you had stolen that as well."

Answer on page 78.

16. Win Princess Rebecca
"Painter B. Rown, you are the only one who managed to get it right. You shall have my lovely daughter." The king froze in horror, for he had just noticed Rown's feet. "This won't do at all," he stammered. "My daughter can not possibly marry a man who goes around with only one sock. I'll give you two minutes to find the other sock, or our deal is off."

Answer on page 78.

17. Beat the Train
"Let's take the steamer," suggested Michael. "It'll be fun."

"No, our friends are expecting us," Michele reminded him. "We can take the steamer on the way back. Now let's see—the train, since it is an hour late, will be at Lakeside at 4 o'clock. The bus, being twice as slow as the train, will take one hour. Since it leaves at 2:08, it should arrive in Lakeside at around 3:08. And that's much earlier than the steamer. Get your suitcase—we'll take the bus."

Michael and Michele had the same type of suitcase: blue with a long red stripe. But Michael's suitcase had gotten mixed up with other luggage coming in from Eaglestone. Can you find it?

Answer on page 78.

18. Solve the Space Snafus
Jack found two green hexagonal frames. The other fourteen were five-sided, or pentagons.

"It seems I have to check every little detail

myself," said Dr. Baker. "The other day two of my workers nearly floated away into space because they didn't attach themselves properly. Come to think of it, I'd better check them now, before it's too late."

Do you want to check them out, too?

Answer on page 78.

19. Fix the Dinosaur

Kirsten put the big white tooth into the mouth of the tyrannosaurus, while Ken discovered that the other parts fit into the head crest and shoulder of the triceratops. They finished their job just as Professor Gruber arrived for the inspection.

"Very good," he said, stroking his beard. Then he pondered, "It is true that we don't know what color the dinosaurs were, but I think you went just a little bit overboard with your paint. For instance, why did you paint this green line all over the body of triceratops?"

"I didn't paint a green line," said Kirsten.

Ken added, "Neither did I."

Well, who did?

Answer on page 78.

20. Spot the Santa

Both Lolly and Robert came to the conclusion that the Santa who was sitting closest to the steps was the only one who fit the bill.

"Excuse me, sir," said Lolly politely, "are you by any chance the real Santa Claus?"

"Sure am, kiddo," said the man.

This made the children immediately suspicious. They thought the real Santa Claus would never use the word "kiddo."

"If you are the real Santa Claus," said Lolly, "then you must be an expert on snowflakes. Tell me what's wrong with the snow crystal decorations up there."

"They look okay to me," said the man.

The children knew that he was an imposter. How did they know?

Answer on page 78.

21. Spot the Glasses

Danny pointed to the tree-fork above where the spectacles had lodged. The alien retrieved them with a stick.

"Thanks, Danny," he said. "And while we're here, may we ask another favor? How

about some fresh water for our goldfish?"

"Help yourself," Danny said. "I'll turn the tap on. Just take the end of the hose and I'll give you all the water you want."

"Very kind of you," said the alien. "But where is the end of the hose?"

Danny laughed. "You have six eyes and you can't even see the end of the hose?"

Can you see it?

Answer on page 78.

22. Why the Majeo?

Patrick and Peggy worked out that the word Majeo was made up of the first letter of each team member's name—Matt, Anita, John, Ellen, and Olga.

"One more thing puzzles me," said Peggy. "Why are the wings painted different colors?"

"Ah, you see," explained Matt, "instead of building two prototypes, we built only one plane, but with two different wings. If the aircraft flies in a left curve, we'll know that the right wing is faster. If it turns right, we'll know that the left wing is better. Clever, isn't it? Look closely and you'll discover that it's not only the color that's different. There are three other things we have changed."

Can you see what they are?

Answer on page 78.

23. Find the Tablet

Ms. Stonnell's assistants found the rest of the tablet in two parts—one under the stairs: and the other under the lid of the sarcophagus. As they put the three pieces together, Ms. Stonnell called out, "Just as I thought! A fish!"

"Why is that of special significance?" asked the assistants.

"Because it was the king's symbol. I believe there must be a box in this tomb that contains the scrolls on which the king kept his diary. It should have the same fish symbol on it. We must find it!"

Can you help?

Answer on page 78.

24. Find the Toothbrush

The witch found the toothbrush on the windowsill. "Here it is," she called out triumphantly. "Now you'll stay and have some candy, won't you?"

"Not on your life," said Ned. "Do you

really think we'd use your toothbrush? Please tell us the way to town and we'll be on our way."

The witch stopped smiling. Stamping her feet, she called out, "I want you to stay! If you don't, I'll put a flat-tire spell on your bikes."

"A flat-tire spell?" laughed Ted, "There's no such thing!"

"There is so," said the witch. "All I have to do is find three animals that rhyme with 'flat,' boil them up in my cauldron, then make you drink the potion."

The boys looked around. They didn't believe in flat-tire spells and they certainly wouldn't have drunk the liquid. But they thought they had better save the three animals from that crazy old woman!

Can you help them find the animals before the witch does?

Answer on page 78.

25. Find the Tragic Mushroom
They found the mushroom directly above the place where Creepy was sitting with his clipboard. As they expected, one of the dwarves would be bitten again! They had better check each item of their clothing before going home! Do you see why?

Answer on page 79.

26. Help the Genie
Rich and Ruthie took the large orange box directly in front of them. It already had the colors green and blue on it. If they could add some red, they would be all right. They remembered seeing a can of red paint. All they had to do was to find it again—plus a paintbrush. Can you help?

Answer on page 79.

27. Lowering the Noonball
Purple Nessie was frightened off by the loud explosion of the balloon, thereby lowering the ball. She had hardly moved two yards when the red lever on top moved as far as it could, and the whole tower came crashing down. All six people scrambled for a lifesaver. Were there enough for all of them?

Answer on page 79.

28. The Disappearing Wallet
Rita had seen a little green hand come from behind the curtain and skillfully remove the wallet from Roger's jacket.

"As far as the tattoo is concerned," she said, "why do you want to remove anything before writing the name of your new girlfriend? There's another way to do it."

Do you know what that is?

Answer on page 79.

29. Find the Leaf
They found such a leaf to the left of the lion's head, only to discover that they forgot the little ukelele that they always used to accompany themselves in the sing-along. One of them had to go find it and bring it back.

Answer on page 79.

30. The Magic Carpet
After looking around, the aliens spotted the same carpet under the yellow-flowering tree. They decided to land their craft on the helipad marked with a big H. But would they find their way from there to the carpet they wanted to buy?

Answer on page 79.

31. Find the Right Berries
They found an edible twinberry between red sections, right on the very top of the plant.

"Just for comparison," suggested the humanoid, "you ought to take a deadly one. As I said, they grow between green sections of the plant. They are hard to find, but if you're a true scientist, you won't give up."

Answer on page 79.

32. Food Festival
The Royal Food Collector made a tour through all of Spreewald, but could have saved himself the trouble. When he came back after two or three hours, he found that the very place where he had landed fitted the description perfectly. Unfortunately, the people there did not understand him.

"Go see Professor Klinkerman," they said. "He speaks all languages. He's easy to find because he's never far from his dog, a white-and-brown one with a black tail."

Answer on page 79.

33. Mixed-Up Times

"Well, I recognize the crablike animals below me. They're trilobites," said Tina. "Prehistoric animals happen to be my hobby. Trilobites were common in the Cambrian Age some 600 million years ago."

"If your hobby were the ancient world," said Gloork, "you'd recognize that owl-like figure beneath you as coming from the Chang Dynasty. It's about 600 years old."

That's two things—here are more:

3 and 4: The *Spirit of St. Louis*, the plane in which Charles Lindbergh crossed the Atlantic in 1928, is giving Roman soldiers the surprise of their lives!

5 and 6: A tank from modern times is being inspected by a group of Crusaders from the Middle Ages.

7: One of the Crusaders is being photographed, and photography wasn't invented until the nineteenth century.

8 to 11: There are items from the twentieth century—a lawnmower, a can, and a bottle, and a book.

12: In the background you'll see the pyramids, which date back thousands of years.

13: Tyrannosaurus Rex is wandering near the pyramids, though he lived many millions of years before they were built.

"You better give your time machine a good checkup," said Gloork. "For instance, are you sure that the red contacts are properly connected to the blue ones? That's a common mistake with time machines, you know."

Answer on page 79.

MORE ANSWERS

1. Find the Thief
The bottle is on the shelf right above the dog and to the left.

2. Find the Sandals
The hairbrush is to the right by the tire and lantern. The mother's bag is on the table.

3. The Exploding Planet
The fuel tanks are hooked up all right.

4. Spot the Getaway Car
The dog is on the grass between the river and the Fairyland sign.

5. Spot the Ring
In his usual style, the jewel thief hid the ring in the flowerpot, the one that is next to the bride. The jewel thief himself is in the fourth row center.

6. Help Ashley Survive
There are ten buttons and ten squirrels.

7. Fish or Chicken?
They had just enough money for the tickets.

8. Help Yill Help Yack
He can do it.

9. Find the Wolf
Yes, he did drop them on his walk. They are under one of the fir trees behind Grandmother's house.

10. Where's the Camera?
The bicycle pump is alongside the sneakers, by the roots of the tree.

11. Find Ginger!
The glove is on a branch of the bush in the yard of the house across the street.

12. Can You Save Your Life?
In addition to the pirate's pants, there are eights on the treasure chest, on separate pieces of treasure, on bars of gold, on the mast of the boat, and on the ropes. How many more eights can you find?

13. Where's the Knife?
The name of the ship was STELLA.

14. Naming the Creature
The snakeweed with the crosses in the middle can be found at the bottom left, in another left-hand group between Hannah and Jessie, and in the group at the right beside the tree.

15. Test the Fiendish Invention
McRob stole the Queen's crown, all right. He left it in plain sight up by the window. A bird is nesting in it.

16. Win Princess Rebecca
The sock is hanging on the railing outside the gatekeeper's house.

17. Beat the Train
Michael's suitcase is on the platform, three bags down from the gray-haired woman.

18. Solve the Space Snafus
Two of the space workers are attached to each other—but not to the space station.

19. Fix the Dinosaur
The mouse did it.

20. Spot the Santa
Real snowflakes always have six points. The real Santa would know that.

21. Spot the Glasses
The end of the hose is almost completely hidden behind the bushes above where the cat is standing.

22. Why the Majeo?
1. The number of wing flaps are different—four on one, three on the other.
2. The colors of the propeller cap are different.
3. The colors on the center of the propeller cap are different.

23. Find the Tablet
The box is underneath the ladder.

24. Find the Toothbrush
1. The cat is sitting on the can of industrial treacle.
2. The rat is at the side of the house.
3. The bat is hanging upside down above the clothesline.

25. Find the Tragic Mushroom
A deadly blue adder is about to crawl into one of the dwarves' boots.

26. Help the Genie
The can of red paint is to their far right, near the box with the fish on it. The paintbrush is near the kids, on the floor of the old truck.

27. Lowering the Noonball
Yes, there were six lifesavers. (One is on the dog's neck.)

28. The Disappearing Wallet
All you have to do to change LIL to NELLY is to add an N at the beginning, change the first L to an E, the I to an L, leave the second L, and add a Y at the end.

29. Find the Leaf
The ukelele is up on the left in the fork of the thick branches of the thorn-vine tree.

30. The Magic Carpet
To get from landing place H to the carpet the aliens want to buy, they can travel along the tops of the walls until they get to the area where the carpet is. Then all they need to do is walk down the steps to get to it.

31. Find the Right Berries
There's a good one at the bottom of the page, right near the tapewormoid.

32. Food Festival
Professor Klinkerman is in a boat with his dog, up near the farm with the sheep and the big pink bush.

33. Mixed-Up Times
Gloork is right. The red A wires are hooked up to red B, instead of being hooked into the blue ones. Blue A wires are hooked up to blue B, and blue B wires are hooked up to blue D, instead of being hooked up to red wires.

INDEX